The LET'S FIND OUT Books

by Martha and Charles Shapp

LET'S FIND OUT ABOUT ANIMAL HOMES
LET'S FIND OUT WHAT'S BIG AND WHAT'S SMALL
LET'S FIND OUT WHAT ELECTRICITY DOES
LET'S FIND OUT ABOUT FIREMEN
LET'S FIND OUT ABOUT HOUSES
LET'S FIND OUT ABOUT INDIANS
LET'S FIND OUT WHAT'S LIGHT AND WHAT'S HEAVY
LET'S FIND OUT ABOUT POLICEMEN
LET'S FIND OUT ABOUT SCHOOL
LET'S FIND OUT WHAT THE SIGNS SAY
LET'S FIND OUT WHAT'S IN THE SKY
LET'S FIND OUT ABOUT THE UNITED NATIONS
LET'S FIND OUT ABOUT WATER
LET'S FIND OUT ABOUT WHEELS

and

LET'S FIND OUT ABOUT SPRING
LET'S FIND OUT ABOUT SUMMER
LET'S FIND OUT ABOUT FALL
LET'S FIND OUT ABOUT WINTER

LET'S FIND OUT ABOUT
FALL

by

MARTHA and CHARLES SHAPP

Pictures by László Roth

FRANKLIN WATTS, INC.
575 Lexington Avenue, New York 22

SBN 531–00021–4

Library of Congress Catalog Card Number: 62-13950
Printed in the United States of America
by The Moffa Press

11

There are four seasons in the year —

winter,

spring,

summer,

and fall.

Some people like winter best.

Some people like spring.

5

Some like summer.

Others like fall best of all.

When is fall?

Fall is when you are back in school after summer vacation.

Fall is when it gets cool.

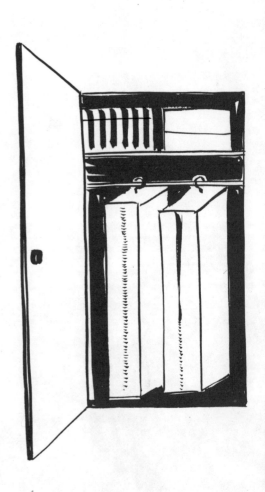

You put away summer clothes and put on warmer clothes.

In the fall the days get shorter and shorter.
You can't play outdoors very long after school.

It gets dark too early.

The sudden frost that comes on a fall night kills many flowers.
One day the flowers are tall and bright.

The next day the flowers are dead.

The leaves of many trees change color in the fall.

In the fall many animals get ready for winter.

The fur on some animals gets thicker.

Some animals put away food for the winter.

Many birds fly away to warmer places.

The frogs go down to the bottom of the pond.

There they sleep all winter.

In the fall the caterpillar makes a cocoon in which it sleeps all winter.
While it sleeps, the caterpillar changes into a moth.

In the spring the moth comes out of the cocoon.

People get ready for winter, too.

Vegetables are picked and put away for winter food.

Fruit is picked for winter food.

Halloween comes in the fall.

35

Thanksgiving Day comes in the fall.
The first Thanksgiving dinner was long ago.

Thanksgiving Day is still celebrated every fall

with a Thanksgiving dinner.

There are four seasons in the year,

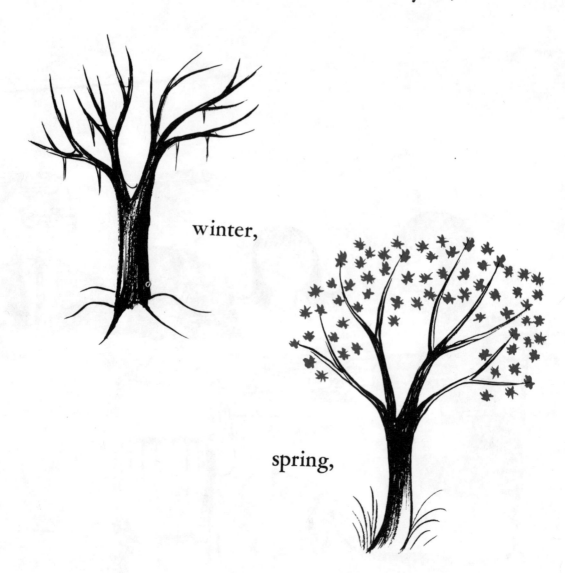

winter,

spring,

summer,

fall.

Which season is the best season of all?

VOCABULARY (100 words)

a	four	pond
after	frogs	put
ago	frost	
all	fruit	ready
and	fur	
animals		school
are	get(s)	season(s)
away	go	shorter
		sleep(s)
back	Halloween	some
best		spring
birds	in	still
bottom	into	sudden
bright	is	summer
	it	
can't		tall
caterpillar	kills	Thanksgiving
celebrated		that
change(s)	leaves	the
clothes	like	there
cocoon	long	they
color		thicker
comes	makes	to
cool	many	too
	moth	trees
dark		
day(s)	next	vacation
dead	night	vegetables
dinner		very
down	of	
	on	warm(er)
early	one	was
every	others	when
	out	which
fall	outdoors	while
first		winter
flowers	people	with
fly	picked	
food	places	year
for	play	you